A big thanks to my family; Mum, Dad, and Joe. Steve, for introducing to this thing called "The Knowledge". Also my call-over partners (Kevin, Julian, and Angus), without your support this life changing journey would have taken far longer!

Tom Hutley is a full time London Black cab driver.

Since completing The Knowledge of London he has continued to study London from a historical perspective, offering extensive tours of the capital.

More information and updates are available at: http://tom.taxi

CONTENTS

Introduction	1
What is The Knowledge?	3
Why become a London cab driver?	7
Getting Started	13
Blue Books	31
Pointing	43
Point to Point	51
Call-over partner	57
Map test	61
Appearances	63
Suburban runs	93
London cab driver	95
Glossary	101
Knowledge schools & resources	105

INTRODUCTION

Graduating from university in 2013 with a first class degree, I had followed the expected paths to a **good** life, but once the academic current had stopped, I was truly lost.

Across a span of a year and a half, I hopped between jobs (three to six months was my average tenure), started my own business and dissolved it, before advancing to a graduate sales job in the City. I worked in the City, so immediately began a flat-share without even considering the direction I was going in. Whilst scouring LinkedIn for prospective cold calling leads, I had an epiphany; selling corporate training business to business wasn't going to lead to a fulfilling life.

So I took the brave decision to stop, strip back my life and simplify, starting from the bottom. Forgetting my past or the fact that I had a degree, I had one aim. How do I make my life more intentional?

By January 2015 I had left the commission enticing sales job in the City and moved back home with my parents. I got a basic retail job and began studying The Knowledge of London in my spare time. I knew from previously having my own business that I enjoyed working for myself. Money was never a huge motivator for me; I knew that if I could work to my own schedule, I could design my life how I see fit.

INTRODUCTION

It was a path like no other, studying from passion and the desire to improve myself rather than just as the means to achieve an academic deadline. Being brutal with my life, I removed the non-essential and questioned what truly mattered to me and what I wanted to achieve. My girlfriend and I soon discovered we were on different paths so we broke up; the game was on, I had all the motivation with the least amount of excuses.

The months flew by, I had soon completed the formative "Blue Books" that are required to study The Knowledge. I was picking up points of interest every day and soon approaching my first exam, "The Map Test". Once that was passed, I progressed onto "appearances", the oral examinations that make The Knowledge so famous. Every day became a balancing act that involved my day job, discovering the streets of London and constantly revising all of this new information. There weren't enough hours in the day to amass all of the information required, but I was hooked. I now knew that completing The Knowledge would lead to the lifestyle I required in life.

In December 2017, after two years and 11 months of intensive study, I received my coveted green badge. I was now a real London cabbie!

In the chapters that follow, I want to share with you why I and many others have opted for the long and arduous study that it takes to become a London cab driver. I will highlight the exact steps you need to take to begin your journey to earn the coveted badge, from the big sacrifices and daily struggles of studying, right through to some of my experiences of what it is like when you are out working in the cab.

WHAT IS THE KNOWLEDGE?

Legend has it, that The Knowledge was created following the Great Exhibition of 1851 in Hyde Park. The Knowledge is the formalised examination process that any aspiring London cab driver must undertake to acquire their badge and, therefore, the right to work as a London hackney carriage driver.

It involves committing to memory 320 standardised runs across the city, then developing a further Knowledge to learn points of interest among the 25,000 streets that exist within the six-mile radius of Charing Cross station that is required for The Knowledge.

It is the toughest taxi test in the world and arguably one of the most brutal examination methods too. With a dropout rate of 80%, it compares with the success rate of becoming a U.S. Navy Seal.

The London cab driver populous floats around the 25,000 mark (21,000 green badges, 4,000 yellow badges). This number fluctuates but is roughly accurate, as those who retire their badge are being replaced by many new cab drivers.

WHAT IS THE KNOWLEDGE?

The Public Carriage Office (PCO) was previously coordinated by the London Metropolitan Police, but has been managed by Transport for London (TfL) since July 2000. TfL is also jointly responsible for London Underground, buses and generally anything to do with the transport infrastructure that exists within the capital.

To learn The Knowledge, there are three key components that you will build up over your years of study.

1. Blue Books
2. Points

---

3. Point to point (which later becomes your appearances).

Blue Books are your routes, your core roads across the city. Think of them as your starting guide to London; they provide a good base knowledge to build upon. Points are your "points of interest", these are locations that a passenger may ask for. Point to point is when you learn to create your own routes based on the start and end point, using nothing but your own mental GPS.

I've placed a line between 1, 2 & 3 because you cannot start point to point without first completing Blue Books and gathering points of interest. When starting out, there are two ways of getting to P2P, these are two school methods: Knowledge Point or WizAnn. I will cover the difference between these methods in later chapters.

This book is also assembled in the order that each relevant process should take place; starting with Blue Books, then Pointing, Point to Point, Map Test and Appearances.

THE LONG ROAD AHEAD

Don't believe that you'll find an easier way to do The Knowledge. Believe me, either of the routes (WizAnn or Knowledge Point) still require lots of hard work and sacrifice!

From my very first Blue Book to working my first shift in the cab, it took me almost three years to complete the task. It's not like an academic degree where you can put off the hard work and then buck up your ideas as the deadline approaches, blagging your way through the exam. To achieve the required standard, The Knowledge is a constant workload. From waking up in the morning to going to bed at night, there are just not enough hours in the day!

I took my study materials on an all-inclusive holiday in the Caribbean and called over every day between 9am and 3pm (believe me, this did not feel like enough). Some of my friends skipped going on holiday altogether and their busy Knowledge schedule meant their home lives were full of tension.

I lost touch with a lot of friends during my experience, as well as my aforementioned girlfriend. You have to learn to make many sacrifices and start saying, "Sorry mate, can't come out for a drink tonight." And all this for the eventual goal of being able to do exactly what you want to in life.

WHAT IS THE KNOWLEDGE?

WHY BECOME A LONDON CAB DRIVER?

Being a London Cab Driver is one of the most unique jobs in the world.

You are your own boss and can work when you want to and for how long you want. Want to go on holiday next week? Do it. Has your boiler broken and you need some extra money to pay for it? Work overtime this week. You can vary your work to whatever the circumstances of your life may be.

For me, I used to despise the hours where I would be at an office job doing "nothing tasks". I had achieved my sales targets, why should I be inclined to do anything else? I remember working in the office on Christmas Eve. As it was B2B (business to business), all the prospective clients and their respective companies had gone home for the holiday break. I was being paid to sit and look busy. It's not that I despised the work, I have quite a high job satisfaction and love the challenges that any job environment provides; it was just how unintentional the work then became. I wanted

WHY BECOME A LONDON CAB DRIVER?

a job where I could appropriate my hours around the life that I wanted to lead. Life first, work second.

This year, I took up snowboarding. It still fascinates me that I can spend a morning on an indoor slope, then hop into my cab and go to work from there! Life first, work second.

I'm currently writing this section of the book whilst sitting in a bar in Berlin. I didn't need to get any time off from my boss and nor do I have a scheduled date when I am expected to return to work. Life first, work second.

Once you have completed The Knowledge, you never have to sit another examination again, as long as you renew your licence every three years (currently £180), and have a medical every five years if you're over 50. You are eligible to rent/own a black cab and work how you want to work.

You could take a year out, travel the world, come back, rent a cab and get straight back to work.

Some drivers are UK ex-pats living in Spain, they come back and rent a cab for the summer or winter months before returning back to Spain. Some work week on week off. Heathrow drivers sleep at the feeder park to catch the first flight, starting their day off. I have stayed in hotels to make the most of a long weekend of working.

I'm never on time to work but I'm also never late. Having a bad day or feeling tired? Come home early, this job works for you.

I can't think of any other job or profession where you can quite literally start and stop when you want to. I've always had to either work for a client or customer. Someone who expects me to open shop at 9am, be on a set at 6am, or a product to be delivered by 6pm that evening. Comparing to those standards, it is an easy and relatively stress-free existence. Yes, you still have to work the hours but it makes a huge difference knowing that you have picked those hours, depending on how you feel.

YOUR LEVEL OF QUALIFICATION

On the surface, telling your friends and family you wish to be a taxi driver sounds hardly like the most fulfilling job in the world. But in truth, you are easily one of the most over-qualified professionals in the world, and as you go about your knowledge journey, you develop a new view on London which later escalates to what I call a Sherlock Holmes-esque style of perception.

You will see ambulances racing across the city and know exactly where they have come from and the likely area they are heading to. You will be equipped to know every single possible route across the city. Just by glancing at the entrance to one road, you will instantly know the possibilities of all the locations and roads that lie beyond it.

Just one single road closure might affect the consecutive streets that you've intended to take, so you have to reassemble another route in your mind on the fly – all this whilst driving and even having a conversation with the passenger in the back! There's no chance to stop and a bad choice of turn can add unnecessary time to the journey.

You are not just a taxi driver, you are a professional navigator; you hold the keys to London in your mind and are an expert geographer of the six-mile radius of Charing Cross station. Best of all, this Knowledge belongs to you; it is your interpretation and you can use it exactly when and how you wish! No-one can ever take that away from you, and let me tell you, it is incredibly liberating to know the ins and outs of one of the world's major cities!

WHO ARE LONDON CAB DRIVERS?

The flexible working nature of the job attracts individuals from various backgrounds. These range from men who have dabbled in various forms of employment before settling for cabbing, to women who want the greatest flexibility for their families.

Firefighters, police officers, sports people – just about anyone and everyone can become a London cab driver for their own benefit. Firefighters can earn extra money around their stationed hours, police officers can top up their pension once retired, and semi-professional sportspeople can supplement their main passion in life.

We're all an interesting bunch, but despite the varied background, one commonality unites us all – The Knowledge.

HOW MUCH CAN I EARN?

The beauty of working for yourself is that your earning potential is only limited by your own hours. The 2017 Channel 4 documentary, *The Knowledge: The World's Toughest Taxi Test*, reveals that a cabbie could potentially earn over £40,000 in a year.

It is wise to treat being a cab driver as a business and not a job. We don't all earn the same money and everyone's expenses will vary, in the same way that one restaurant chain is prosperous whilst another down the street may struggle. It's the same business but their different modes of operating can yield different results.

People in employed backgrounds like to look at the big figures, but the advertised salaries on job boards are before tax. In the cab, turnover can look very impressive, but factor in your weekly cab rental, fuel bill and tax provisions, and that number will be significantly impacted.

You also have to factor in that you won't have any holiday pay, sick pay or retirement options provided for you. I'm not trying to put a downer on it, but for every positive that this job offers, there is also a negative.

For me, the biggest benefit is being time independent and being able to earn whenever it's suitable for me. It's not going to make you a millionaire but it can certainly improve your quality of life and you will earn a good living from it.

If you want to earn mega-money, this profession probably isn't for you. If you want to work for yourself, control your hours and have a good standard of living, I believe that being a London cab driver is a pretty effective way of achieving those aims.

GREEN BADGE OR YELLOW BADGE?

In London there are two types of taxi licence; Green Badge (All London) and Yellow Badge (Sector specific). The main

WHY BECOME A LONDON CAB DRIVER?

difference between the two is that Green Badges can cover all of London, if you have hailed a taxi in Central London, this will be a Green badge driver. This is the most sought after badge, and what we will be covering in this book.

Yellow badges still undergo The Knowledge but learning a particular borough/suburb of London. Some people opt for this badge as it generally takes less time to complete. They can only accept street hails from within their designated borough. More information on this badge is available on the TfL website.

GETTING STARTED

HOW MUCH DOES IT COST?

The great thing about The Knowledge is that anyone can start as it's relatively inexpensive – just your time, fuel and a few study books are needed. The only other essential is a can-do attitude and a good routine!

At some point, you will need to apply for the Knowledge through TfL, which includes a criminal disclosure check and a medical check from a GP.

This is to get you on the TfL system, so they can recognise how many people may be running their Blue Books and will need to be examined at some point in the future. Once you've applied, TfL will send you a guide about what to expect in the process (such as sitting a voluntary assessment once you have run 80 runs). This initial application doesn't include any exam fees.

I would hold fire on applying directly to TfL until you have been on a few runs to see if the process is for you. You do not need to apply for The Knowledge to begin learning your

GETTING STARTED

Blue Books. TfL also give you a two-year deadline before sitting your first exam (it is recommended that you have completed all the Blue Books and obtained at least 2,000 points). If you cannot commit to starting your exams during this time and you are not ready, I definitely would not even attempt the exam!

If you overrun the two-year deadline, you will have to reapply and pay the associated fees once more!

The only reason you need to apply from the very beginning is if you have a criminal or medical record which might create a problem with being licensed. You will only get to know this by contacting TfL directly or submitting your application with the completed criminal record and medical check.

To apply officially though TfL you need to be a minimum of 18 years old, but you can start running Blue Book runs before this age. Also be aware that you cannot start driving a cab until you are 21 (some knowledge boys/girls complete The Knowledge and have to wait until their 21st birthday to start working).

I started by purchasing Blue Book 1 and running the first few runs in my car. It's best to see how these go before investing any more time and money. It is hard and daunting to start with. Keep the progress small at first, so as not to deter yourself.

I have outlined all of the fixed costs below (non-negotiable items that have to be paid for to get your licence).

Fixed Costs

DBS disclosure application (first)	£57
Medical assessment	£80
TfL Application fee	£120
Knowledge of London written examination (Map test)	£200
Knowledge of London appearance fees (one-off)	£400
Issue of badge fee	£180
DBS disclosure application (2nd to issue badge)	£57
Medical assessment (if over 50, when completing The Knowledge)	£80
Approx. total costs	£1,117- £,1174

*Costs correct at time of print April 2019

GETTING STARTED

Be aware that there can be a large space of time between these costs; for instance, after applying it is usually a minimum of a year before you are ready for your map test and then further appearances.

Appearances usually last for a minimum of a year and you will only need to pay the issue or badge fee once they are completed.

Here's an example of my fixed costs broken down.

2015	DBS, TfL Application, Medical	£257
2016	Written exam, appearance fees	£600
2017	Issue of badge, DBS	£237

The fixed costs remain the same, but when you have to pay them depends on your progress.

Flexible costs

Flexible costs are items that are variable to your budget or Knowledge journey. These include things such as books, maps, fuel, modes of transport, getting to and from the exam centre, etc.

- To ensure your knowledge journey doesn't come to a halt, I would strongly recommend planning and budgeting how much it will cost you for the following:
- Weekly transport costs (how many times a week will you complete runs or go pointing?)
- How often will you need to buy knowledge books or resources? Will you buy new ones or reuse old material?

- Is your car/bike reliable? Will you be able to afford to repair it if it breaks down?
- Will you be joining a knowledge school or have a subscription to daily point sheets?

Be realistic with these expectations. I would have loved to travel into London five days a week to improve my Knowledge process but realistically, I could only afford three days a week. You might find that one to two days may be more ideal for your budget. There isn't a right amount of time, but if you can't afford to keep up the routine, it could seriously hinder your progress.

CAR VS. BIKE

I live approximately 40 miles from London and did a 50/50 split of The Knowledge in my car and on my motorbike (a Suzuki Bandit 600 to survive driving down the M11). I generally used the car in winter and motorbike in the warmer months when there was better weather.

Both have their advantages and drawbacks. The car was brilliant at 3am, with the heaters blowing and coffee in the cup holder, whilst the motorbike was incredible in town and for cutting through traffic.

So long as you come to London at the right time (early mornings/late evenings), you can dodge the majority of traffic. You will inevitably find some traffic, but you can make this beneficial by using the time to glance at the buildings and find new points of interest.

Not one mode of transport works any better than the other, some Knowledge boys/girls have completed The Knowledge using just a bicycle! Just remember, the best vehicle to do The Knowledge on/in is the one that actually goes out and does The Knowledge. It can be very easy to think that you need a smaller car or a faster scooter, but anything does the job. I had a 17-year-old Ford Focus!

COMMON EXCUSES

I live too far from London

This is all down to your personal circumstances and what you consider to be a viable commute. Imagine you get your badge and start working as a London cab driver tomorrow, would you be prepared to commute five days a week from your location? A good knowledge schedule is almost like being a working cab driver, as you have to regularly commute into London to learn the streets and places.

With regards to distance making the process of getting your badge easier, I believe there is zero advantage to be gained from living in London or living out of it, other than the time allowance. When you are in the appearance room, you have only your memory to rely upon, so whether you live across the road or 100 miles away, you have no direct advantage. I would even argue that those who have not lived or worked in London stand a greater chance. As they have not formulated any pre-existing routes or assumptions in their head, they will start from scratch, learning London by the map.

I have a bad memory

Unless you have a physical/mental condition that prohibits you from formulating new memories, I believe we all have the capacity to learn and store all the required information for The Knowledge.

If I say the words, *"Never Eat Shredded Wheat,"* most of you will remember it as the acronym for remembering North/East/South/West (clockwise) on a compass face.

WASP, for instance, is a section of roads to cut across Chelsea into South Kensington. Walpole St, Anderson St, Sloane Ave, Pelham St.

Along your Knowledge journey, you will make many acronyms and word associations that will mentally trigger in your brain. Recently, a customer in the cab asked me for Micklewhaite Road and he was astounded that I knew it. This is a handy cut through from North End Road to Lillie Road, and I was able to picture it as I always formulate a mental image of my friend, whose surname is Meiklejohn. Points of interest are relatively easy to remember. If I say London Eye, you instantly have an image of it which triggers the location and, therefore, the road. Adding in your own visual clues makes this same memory process a breeze with roads.

I highly recommend a Google search on the subject of memorisation as a few simple techniques will make the process much easier and efficient.

It will take too long

Unless it consumes the remainder of your existence on the Earth, time should never be a deciding factor.

One quote that turned my mind off of this excuse was "time will pass anyway". If it takes three to five years, you will still age during that time. I didn't want to look at myself in five years' time and think, "Oh, I really should have got up and started The Knowledge."

Besides, the other motivating factor is to take as little time as possible. As the motorbike racer and TV personality, Guy Martin, says: "Do it once, do it right."

"THE BEST TIME TO PLANT A TREE WAS 20 YEARS AGO, THE SECOND BEST TIME IS NOW." CHINESE PROVERB

I haven't got time

I personally believe this is one of the weakest excuses of all, comparable to when people say, "I haven't got time to go to the gym."

Reading between the lines, whenever I hear this statement, my brain flips the script to reveal the true meaning as: "I haven't got enough control of my life to schedule the appropriate time to complete this task."

THE KNOWLEDGE

It is ultimately your life; yes, everyone's circumstances are different but we make the best out of these given conditions.

Those who have managed to maintain a solid gym routine in their life will know that having a busy life is often the best way to fit these actions in. Here's an example.

Have you ever woken up on a Saturday morning, knowing that you have a day off and just a couple of tasks to do? You might need to take some rubbish to the tip, get new tyres on the car, and buy a pair of jeans. With this abundance of time, you know that you have the entire day to space out those three tasks. However, with the correct scheduling, you can easily manage all of those tasks around a working day, often completing them in far less time. Let's say you go to the tip before work, get the tyres changed at lunch and buy your jeans before you get home for dinner. You have set yourself clear deadlines for the task to be done, without the unlimited potential the weekend offers, so you can either get the task done or it has to be skipped.

Note: This has become really prominent now. I've actually found that since getting my badge, I am in some ways less effective without a routine/accountable time to get to work to satisfy my employment criteria (say 9 o' clock). Without an imposed deadline that governs my livelihood, I can let small tasks slip, taking a little longer than needs be, which for the reason outlined above, clearly isn't a good thing.

Impose deadlines, work with your constrictions, they will make you a better person!

GETTING STARTED

Minicabs/Driverless cars taking over.

The London Hackney carriage has existed in some form for over four centuries. The Knowledge has existed for over 150 years. In a constantly updating city, the population, the economy and employment all increase, so there is always a need for professional drivers in London.

I see driverless cars (in my opinion, decades away at the minimum) as a bigger threat than the ride-hailing apps and minicabs. Put it this way, there is always a cheaper competitor in every industry, it's like trying to compare EasyJet with First Class on Virgin Atlantic, McDonald's vs. Gordon Ramsay (I'm certain he's not losing sleep when McDonald's launch a new burger). In the words of Richard Branson, "If you can't do it cheaper, do it better."

Uber run on unsustainable pricing models; these are not cheap, they are a loss leader. Yes, good value for the rider, but not sustainable for the driver and, arguably, even the company. There is only so long a company providing a product so cheaply can survive, look at the recent collapse of Poundworld. Eventually, minicab apps will need to raise their prices to provide a sustainable living. Ultimately, their future is less predictable than taxi drivers.

Private hire drivers sometimes study The Knowledge to become Black cab drivers.

Black cab drivers don't become private hire drivers.

HOW LONG DOES IT TAKE?

You can't fail The Knowledge, but you can give up.

THE KNOWLEDGE

At the time of writing, the average length of time to complete The Knowledge is three to five years. Some young bright sparks have completed it in two years with the record now standing just below two years. Some people take up to seven years. A lot of this time is down to the way the examination process is conducted and how you progress (see appearances).

- Complete Blue Book 1 whilst collecting points
- Stage 1 - Sit voluntary assessment
- Complete the remaining Blue Books
- Get a total of 2,000-3,000 Points
- Stage 2 - Sit Map Test
- Start Stage 3 - Appearances (56's)
- Stage 4 - 28's
- Stage 5 - 21's
- Stage 6 - Suburbs
- Badge and cab driver

This was the timeline of my Knowledge progress

- December 2014 - Started Blue Book 1
- May 2015 - Started Blue Book 2 (began pointing alongside Blue Books)
- September 2015 - Sat Voluntary Assessment
- October 2015 - Started Blue Book 3
- February 2016 - Started Blue Book 4
- June 2016 - Finished Blue Book 4
- August 2016 - Sat Map Test
- November 2016 - First Appearance (56's)
- May 2017 - Drop to Stage 4 (28's)
- August 2017 - Drop to Stage 5 (21's)

GETTING STARTED

- November 2017 - Last Appearance Handshake (moved onto Suburbs)
- December 2017 - Completed suburbs and got my badge

In total, I had 13 appearances.

Due to the up-and-down nature of the exams, it can be very hard to predict how long it will take to complete The Knowledge process. The appearance process can sometimes be likened to a game of snakes and ladders, whereby successive failures will send you back to the preceding stage. I studied very hard to minimise my chances of getting a D on appearances. I wanted to ensure that I got through as quickly as possible in order to minimise the overall length of my studying. My tip to get through it as quickly as possible is to have a strong and reliable schedule.

WHAT DO I NEED?

The non-negotiable items in completing The Knowledge are as follows:

- A mode of transport to do runs/pointing (car, scooter, pushbike)
- Blue Book runs (these can be purchased from a school or borrowed from a friend)
- A London A-Z wall map (some go extra-large, I was more comfortable with the standard size)

Aside from notebooks, pens and other stationery, these are the core minimal items required to get through The

Knowledge. As you progress you may find it beneficial to obtain the following:

- A school membership - Enables you to mix with more Knowledge students, learn more lines and take advantage of regular classes/free point sheets
- Daily point sheets - If you can't get to a school regularly enough, daily point sheets will show you what questions have been asked by examiners
- Cross Sections/Missing Piece Runs - These runs focus on intricate roads/streets that are not covered by the blue books. I would say the City and West End runs are very beneficial, even when you are out in the cab
- Football Runs - These runs are designed to help you to see long lines across the map, using large fixed points of interest; in this case, football stadiums.
- A point/run management system - This could be some specific mobile apps or just humble notebooks, which you use to constantly refer back to and revise your runs and points.

Like going to the gym, start out small. If you buy a new scooter, with all the warm waterproof clothing, it's not going to progress you along The Knowledge any faster. In the same way that buying gym clothing and a big stack of dietary supplements isn't going to get you in great shape. You still need to put the work in, regardless of what materials you have.

Once you have committed and made The Knowledge a reliable routine, buying extra pieces can be a good incentive to keep you going but just remember, it won't do the work for you.

I would also recommend going to a local Knowledge school. All Knowledge school's offer an introduction talk about starting The Knowledge (usually free of charge). It can be great to see many people working away, so you can see what is ahead of you, and hear people's perspectives on how to go about things the right way. I had nearly completed Blue Book 1 before I heard about penning or even going pointing. It was only when I went to the intro talk at the London Knowledge School in Grays that this process became much clearer, and I'm very glad I took the opportunity as it shaped my Knowledge journey from that point on.

ARE THERE ANY PREREQUISITES FOR THE KNOWLEDGE?

There is absolutely no previous requirement needed for The Knowledge. You don't even need to come from a driving background or have a driving licence to pass The Knowledge (of course, you will require one if you wish to drive passengers for a living).

The Knowledge is one of the only professions in the world where it is "what you know", not "who you know" that accelerates you in the process.

You could have an extensive lineage of cab drivers in your family, be degree educated or even related to the Royal family and it would make no difference – nothing can gain you an advantage for The Knowledge of London.

CAN I DO IT ALONGSIDE MY JOB?

Unless you are incredibly fortunate to have savings set aside, most knowledge students juggle studying alongside full-time jobs.

How they do this differs and depends on individual circumstances. Stationed firefighters often have down times at work when they can call over their runs. People who are already self-employed can shift their work hours to ensure they have enough time to study. I worked five days a week in retail and squeezed in The Knowledge around the times when I worked.

It doesn't matter what you do in life, you will still feel as though there aren't enough hours in each day to accommodate the enduring task of study.

HOW HARD IS IT TO DO THE KNOWLEDGE?

I modestly tell friends and customers in the cab that The Knowledge isn't hard to do; it is juggling the rest of your life that is the hard bit. Looking back on it now, it is not only a mental struggle, it takes its toll on you physically.

I remember being about 30 runs into my knowledge journey, trying to find a petrol station in Muswell Hill at 11pm. I could barely see through my rain covered helmet visor, and I had to have my visor open so I could see behind the fogged lens. My eyes were barely open, squinting to keep the rain out, in my last attempt to achieve visibility. My Goretex Ultra winter frost proof motorbike gloves were soaked through, my fingertips freezing, and on top of that, I still needed to ride almost an hour in these cold conditions up the M1, knowing that my already cold fingers would be subjected to a windchill of minus 11 degrees.

These are the true struggles of The Knowledge. Your friends and family will envision you going up and down Oxford Street or around Buckingham Palace on your scooter, happily being able to note all of the points of interest. It couldn't be any further from the truth; this is probably one area where you spend the least amount of time on The Knowledge!

I'd be in bed sometime after 1am, my ears still ringing from the noise of the wind that crept into my helmet from the long motorbike ride home. I'd have six hours of sleep and then it would be back to my nine-six job. It was okay, you'd say; after all, I could catch up with friends that evening. Nope, after a desperate scramble home from work, I'd wolf the dinner down, whilst simultaneously watching the last 10 minutes of *The Chase* on ITV (my only regular TV exposure on The Knowledge). It was then up to the bedroom and I'd be in front of the map, cramming every hour until I couldn't go on any more, only to wake up and do it all over again the next day.

Your dreams will soon become complex road networks, areas of London that don't exist and manifest themselves into your subconscious mind. The Knowledge isn't just a waking nightmare; it's even there during the most sacred point of your life, your sleep! Countless times, I've dreamed of being in an appearance and the examiner asking you point after point, only to drop every single one (sometimes, these nightmares happen in real life too!).

If you're on The Knowledge and it hasn't happened yet, it will. It has to take over your life before you can take over it!

Having completed a three-year university degree (First class with honours), I can easily say that the Knowledge far surpasses the degree in terms of intensity. Whilst I completed both in similar time spans, I feel that the tenacity I adopted for The Knowledge meant I could have completed two degrees simultaneously!

Say goodbye to birthdays, Christmas, drinking, TV, holidays and any form of fun. Life's pleasures now become short-lived, as there's only so long you can go without studying before your brain tells you that must get back to work. This is the real day-to-day life of being on The Knowledge.

There is no finish date or graduation date. They say there is a badge for everyone on The Knowledge, you just have to work for it. No-one fails The Knowledge, they just give up. Even up until the very last hurdle, you will doubt yourself every step of the way.

"IN LIFE YOU CAN WIN OR LOSE. IDEALLY, YOU WANT TO WIN QUICKLY, BUT WE'LL ALSO ACCEPT WINNING SLOWLY. IF YOU ARE GOING TO LOSE, LOSE QUICKLY. NEVER LOSE SLOWLY."

GETTING STARTED

BLUE BOOKS

Blue Books (BB's) are the first step that every aspiring cab driver takes to earn their coveted badge. There is no relevance or meaning to the name of these books (in fact, decades ago they used to be pink!). The Blue Books are referred to as your bible on The Knowledge by most people, as they build up your general geographical knowledge of London.

In total, there are 320 Blue Book runs. To make this less daunting, most knowledge schools split these into four books, each containing 80 runs.

Even if you have an extensive Knowledge of London, or have driven around the city for years (you may be able to do this without a sat nav already), Blue Books are still your starting point. This is **not** a step that you can skip or compromise on.

Blue Books feature multiple "runs", essentially driving routes from one point of interest to another, which are studied in conjunction with an A-Z map of London. When penned up on the map, your Blue Book run should be the most direct line between the start and end point.

BLUE BOOKS

To learn any Blue Book run, you will need to do the following:

1. Ride/drive the route
2. Call the run - Knowledge boys and girls do this during and after riding the route.
3. Pen the run - This is done once you arrive back home, pen the route on your map.

Riding and Learning Blue Book runs build up the following:

- Visual knowledge - Physically riding/driving the routes so that you can see them on a street level. This is the most direct experience as a working cab driver.
- Road names - You will need to orally call these and commit all of them to memory. Fluency is key, your Blue Books will become your bible.
- Map Knowledge - Penning allows you to see the route on the map, this is very important. On The Knowledge, we are judged on our ability to visualise/call the straightest route on the map. You might not drive this route because of traffic lights etc. but The Knowledge process is designed to demonstrate that you know the map like the back of your hand.

Going forward you need to:

- Call the run - If your call-over partner asks you to call over Blue Book run #1 Manor House Station -

THE KNOWLEDGE

Gibson Square you should be able to do so fluently, road by road, out loud.
- Visualise the run - In your head, you should be able to see the streets and junctions on the route. Over time, you develop the shape of the line across the map, further strengthening your knowledge.

Starting the Blue Books can be seen as a huge hurdle when starting out, but don't be afraid, it does take time to commit the roads and streets to memory. My advice is to take it slow on the first few runs and only do one or two runs on your first day. You may find that you want to go back and rerun the route to cement it better in your mind.

Like a good diet, gym programme or budget, the results most certainly do not come overnight. Keep your progress small and incremental. Blue Books will become your alphabet or dictionary to how you see London. You will constantly refer back to them so it is important to focus on quality, not quantity.

Calling over/penning your routes at home is as important as going out and running them. I would ensure that the run sticks firmly into your memory before you go out and learn more, so call over whenever you can. Eventually, you will be calling multiple Blue Book runs every day! This becomes an essential part of the schedule. Here's an example of my schedule I had when starting out:

- Sunday am - Ride runs 1 and 2
- Sunday 3pm - Pen and call runs 1 and 2
- Sunday 6pm - Call runs 1 and 2
- Monday am - Call all runs
- Monday pm - Pen and call all runs
- Tuesday am - Call all runs

BLUE BOOKS

- Tuesday pm - Call all runs
- Wednesday am - Ride runs 3 and 4
- Wednesday pm - Pen runs 3 and 4. Call runs 3 and 4
- Wednesday pm - Call all runs

From this schedule, you can see how I made sure my previous runs were fluent before going out and starting new runs. You will also notice how my calling schedule was gradually building.

Penning runs can take some time. I used to pen the run on my map, take a photo of it, then going forward, I could refer to that image as my penned run. I could merely look at a photo of a line drawn on a map and know which of the 320 Blue Book runs it was!

I would recommend making a flashcard system as you build up the number of runs in your memory or purchasing an app to store these for you. WizAnn has a specific run app for storing your runs. You can mark the runs you find more difficult to remember, and this will remind you to revise them more often.

It is also important to call your runs out in a different order to how they appear in the book. Our brain likes to cheat and build up patterns of repetition, so if you always call the runs in the same order, you will struggle if someone gives you a run out of sequence.

Above all, the best thing you can do is get a call-over partner (or multiple call-over partners). I will go into more detail about the benefits of a call-over partner later in the book but essentially, you want to find someone else doing the Knowledge who will help test you on your runs and calling. You can ask a friend or family member to test you on some routes but be warned, as the months go on, they will find the process quite boring and will have less motivation to spot any mistakes you might make.

Keeping motivated

Once you get the hang of driving/riding the streets, completing runs, memorising and calling runs, you will be able to start to forecast how long it will take you to complete the Blue Books based upon your progress.

For instance, if you are able to do around nine runs a week (three an evening, three evenings times a week) when starting out, you could complete Blue Book 1 in just under nine weeks. Times that by four and add in a couple of weeks as a contingency, you could look at completing all 320 runs in 38 weeks. Also, as you progress into later books and start to reuse and cross familiar roads, making your runs more efficient, you may find you can do 12 runs a week by BB4, making the goal of nine months even more achievable.

By the time I got mid-way through BB2, this tight schedule was a huge motivator for me. Completing BB1 was an unmotivated slog, I would do a few runs at the weekend, maybe revise a bit in the week, then contemplate running more at the weekend.

Having a regular routine and clear end goal in sight makes this process incredibly easy. Imagine knowing that you could go to the gym three times in a week and within three-quarters of a year you would have the exact body composition you could dream of. Look at your Blue Book's in this way, stick to your schedule, run them well and before you know it you will have a pretty solid understanding and knowledge of London's roads.

Running runs backwards?

Some people believe it is worthwhile to learn all of the Blue Book runs backwards. Whilst this would most certainly be beneficial, I personally didn't do this for a few reasons.

First off, once you have completed your Blue Books that isn't the end of those roads. For instance, you will have to use and travel across those roads when pointing, sometimes in the wrong direction. Always keep a look out for restrictions when travelling around as you will often find the roads are lenient in one direction, but there may be a restriction in the opposite direction.

In Camden, for instance, I never understood why you cannot turn left into Kentish Town Road from Hawley Road. Left turns are usually less obstructive to traffic than right turns, but you should never assume anything with roads until you have been there and physically seen the signage.

Can't I just use Google Street View to complete all the runs?

Have you ever looked at photos and Street View before going on a holiday, only to get there and find that it looks and feels completely different? When we are driving somewhere, there is a lot of information we take in visually. This is due to the depth and scale of actually being there.

I've used street view when pointing, to assess whether I can use a road junction to catch a turn when leaving a certain building. Often it looks more than doable until I actually go to the location and realise that Google's wide-angle lens has distorted the image, revealing that the manoeuvre would be illegal in real life.

In the same way that most people find the best way to learn how to do something is to physically do it, physically driving the route mentally fixes itself in your head. After all, your job is to drive the streets of London, so if you can't do it in practice you're probably not fit to do it as a profession.

London is always constantly updating, even as a driver who works five days a week, I come across changes I was unaware of that have been in place for weeks or months. Google Street View can take years to update in certain areas. Knowledge examiners also test Knowledge students on the roads that have recently changed to ensure the candidate is keeping up to date with the capital. As a Knowledge student, you should take immense pride in the fact that you are the most informed about the roads and streets that make up the capital.

Don't use a Sat Nav

This might sound incredibly obvious but when you are out learning runs and points, do not fall prey to using a sat nav to navigate into and out of London.

The ultimate key to The Knowledge is understanding the relationship of London; for example, where does Finsbury Park sit in relation to Highbury? Highgate to Camden? Waterloo to Dulwich? When you use a sat nav you don't mentally engage your brain with these relationships. Throughout your knowledge journey, you should always question yourself in this way. You are assembling London into your head, and so you should be able to point in any direction and understand which areas of London lie beyond it.

WHICH KNOWLEDGE SCHOOL?

There are several Knowledge schools based in and outside of London. Some are weekly meet-ups for calling over, whilst others are full-time establishments that produce their own school material (such as Knowledge Point, WizAnn, and Eleanor Cross).

When completing Blue Books there are generally two methodologies to take.

KNOWLEDGE POINT

This is considered to be the original way of doing The Knowledge as outlined by The Public Carriage Office. When you begin Blue Books, you will simultaneously collect points of interest, i.e. BB1, Run No. 1. You will collect four points near to Manor House Station and four points near to Gibson Square.

Advantages

- Once you have completed all your runs, you are immediately ready to start P2P.
- Pointing whilst running BB's can build up your area Knowledge much quicker.

Disadvantages

- Your daily workload can seem a lot more intense.

WIZANN

With this method, you focus only on completing the Blue Books first. Once you have completed all 320 runs you will then begin pointing.

Advantages

- Your daily workload looks simpler. Initially, you only need to revise your runs.
- When pointing you are less intimidated by roads as you have learnt them from the Blue Book already.

Disadvantages

- Once you have finished Blue Books you have to start pointing, which can feel like starting from the beginning again.

Both methodologies lead to the same end goal, and I would argue that neither is quicker or easier than the other. WizAnn can be a very nice way of dipping your toe into The Knowledge world. It is also good for those doing it with limited home time. Neither methodology is set in stone, as you begin learning runs you might start to add pointing to your daily Blue Book journey.

BLUE BOOKS

I completed my Blue Books and Pointing via Knowledge Point, while my call over partner did his through WizAnn. We both got our badges eventually.

CALL A BOOK A DAY

There is a general consensus among most knowledge students to call a book a day. In order to retain our fluency and road knowledge, we always focus on calling an entire Blue Book – that's 80 runs in one day.

Once you're fluent, this practice is usually achievable in under an hour, but breaking up the process across the day is even easier.

Wake up - call 20 runs
Lunch break - call 20 runs
Get home - call 20 runs
Before bed - call 20 runs

These are best practised out of order to ensure you can pull road names and routes from random parts of your memory, as I've already stated. If you have compiled photos of your penned runs, it is even better if you can call from those. This not only strengthens your oral knowledge, but also your visual knowledge.

Always ensure you call aloud, confidently and fluently. Blue Books are a training exercise. Some roads can be hard to pronounce, so by calling aloud time and time again, you are reinforcing your fluency to call that road. Think of it like a foreign language, you cannot learn or speak the language if you don't orally recite the words.

Remember, there is no stated rule that you have to call a Blue Book a day, it is just a general practice that many Knowledge students adhere to in order to retain their fluency.

Recap
- Blue Books are the starting point of The Knowledge, effectively your alphabet of London
- Blue Books build a good Knowledge of London prior to Point to Point
- Blue Books are used right until the final stages in order to retain your fluency in calling roads.

BLUE BOOKS

POINTING

Pointing is the process of finding points of interest within London and committing them to memory.

Below, I have outlined what may constitute as a point of interest:

Train stations, hotels, restaurants, police stations, hospitals, pubs, clubs, bars, churches, synagogues, squares, theatres, embassies, government buildings, famous landmarks, schools, shops, offices, gardens, cemeteries, crematoriums, swimming pools, gyms, ambulance stations, industrial estates, and so on.

These are anywhere a paying passenger may want to go. Make no excuses, examiners will test you on the most obscure locations, as will passengers. Here are some examples of what the examiners asked me on The Knowledge:

- Cottons Rumshack Notting Hill
- Arnold Circus
- Theatre Royal Drury Lane Stage Door
- Warren House
- Aston Martin Clothing Store
- Soho Parish Primary School
- John Lewis Collections Point

POINTING

- Nelson Square
- Wellington Square
- Dominican Embassy
- The Dog's Trust - Asked from Battersea Dogs and Cats Home
- The Half Moon Pub
- Hurlingham Yacht Club
- Putney Library
- Hyde Park Square
- Observatory Gardens
- Jamie Oliver's 15
- Victoria Secrets
- Hanover Primary School
- Almeida Theatre
- Rosemary Branch Theatre
- Cherry Duck Studios
- Bow Quarter Apartments
- The Institute of Directors

There really is no limit to what point you can be asked in an appearance. Passengers can be more forgiving in what they ask you and you can ask for what street. However, with an examiner, you are expected to know with confidence.

Whilst the main piece of knowledge with regards to pointing is to identify which street the point is on, the most important thing is to understand exactly **where** and **how** this point occupies the street. It is the real key to pointing.

Let's use the example of The Institute of Directors. A quick Google search will tell you that this is on Pall Mall. Sounds fine, I've come from Observatory Gardens (West London), trundling along Piccadilly, right St James's St, L Pall Mall, Institute of Directors on your right (Set down on right - SDOR).

THE KNOWLEDGE

If you did this in an exam setting (appearance) you will be scored a big fat 0 out of a possible 10. And no, it's not golf, we want as high a score as possible.

Having properly pointed the Institute of Directors, it is true the doors/entrance is on Pall Mall south side (SS), but there is a solid kerb/central reservation blocking us from setting on the right-hand side. Part of the pointing process is to learn every eventuality of setting/leaving a point (examiners will sometimes ask for a point to be LOL only, despite no physical restrictions). Because of the central reservation, we know that the IoD is SDOL/LOL only (set down on left/left on left only), so we have to find a logical way of approaching the point from the east. In this instance, I would use the following:

To set IoD from the West
Pall Mall, L Regent St, St James's, R Jermyn St, R Haymarket, R Pall Mall, SDOL.

To Leave IoD to head East
LOL Pall Mall, R Regent St, St James's, R Jermyn St, R Haymarket, L Pall Mall East.

This kind of logic needs to be applied to every single point of interest. This is not only necessary for the exam setting, but it's also applicable to driving the cab. Sometimes, busy traffic will make it impossible to turn right or do a U-turn, so we need to have a "turnaround" in mind. Or when we're setting a passenger in a wheelchair, the disabled ramp is on the left side of the cab. For this reason, a SDOL is what we always need to aim for.

Some points are off a main road and the challenge can be learning the intricate streets that lead to that point. Take

Putney Animal Hospital on Clarendon Drive SW15 as an example. It is off of Lower Richmond Road, but to satisfy the examiner you will need to learn the exact order of streets to set it exactly.

Putney Bridge, R Lower Richmond Rd, L Weiss Rd, R Felsham Rd, L Charlwood Rd, R Lacy Rd, L Charlwood Rd, R Clarendon Drive, SDOR.

You and your call-over partner may approach the same problem in different ways. Stick to what works for you, make a mnemonic and best of all, keep it simple.

An example of a mnemonic my call-over partner and I used was: **K**eep **E**verything **L**egal **B**oy

This was used when leaving Camberwell Green Magistrates Court to get back onto the main Camberwell Road.

LOL D'Eynsford Rd, (Keep) L Kimpton Rd, (Everything) L Elmington Rd, (Legal) R Lomond Grove, (Boy), L Bowyer Place.

For every point of interest you go and find, you should know exactly how to set and leave it. If you can pull a point (name what street/road the point is on) in the chair, but can't call your way out of it, expect a 0 for that run!

HOW DO I FIND NEW POINTS?

Most Knowledge schools generate point lists and packs. Generally, these are lists of points ordered by postcode and how frequently they have been asked in an exam setting. These are a very good starting point as it is essential to learn the most commonly asked points; train stations, hotels, restaurants etc. As you progress through the point sheets you will be searching for the most obscure and least asked points.

When you are driving/riding around London, pay attention to all of the buildings. Is there a queue of people outside it? Has the building got a name? Is there a flag/logo hanging up? Does the building look interesting? Make a note of it, research it, ask the security. All of these are clues that the building may have an interesting purpose.

On my introductory Knowledge talk at The Public Carriage Office, one examiner said, "There's no such thing as a hard point, just ones that you don't know."

POINTING FROM SHEETS

Daily point sheets are a good way to go and find points that have actually been asked by an examiner, but proceed with caution here. Remember, these are only the points that have been remembered by the candidate in the exam room, chances are the examiner will have asked plenty more points.

My general rule when going to find points from a sheet was to have a look around the area and find items that are next door or in the same street, as there is a chance the examiner may have asked about them, or will have asked them if you didn't know the first point.

For example, Lock and Co Hatters on St James's St. If you look up and down the street, you have John Lobb shoes and D.R. Harris the chemists on the same side. Many of these establishments will often share the same setting/leaving rules, so it can be an easy way to bag more points of interest.

Three of the points given to me in my final Knowledge exam were points that had never been asked previously, so they would have never been seen on a point sheet. I only knew them as I had seen an interesting looking building or establishment and noted it down.

Remember that examiners might ask something topographical or current. As I write this, we are currently in a climactic point of Brexit, so it's worth doing the homework and finding out where points such as "Europe House" are. The idea is to become as immersed and interested as possible. You are, after all, a student of London.

REVISING POINTS

You'll be glad to know that points of interest generally stick in your memory far more easily than roads. This is because it can be very hard to visualise a road, whereas a point such as the Brazilian embassy will have the national flag hanging outside it so you can associate this memory with a visual cue.

I used to revise my points using flashcards. Some Knowledge students have a physical box of cards, but I used an app (Anki) so that I could revise wherever I went.

Flashcards are quite a simple idea. You write the name of the point of interest on one side (say the London Coliseum), and on the other side you write the name of the street/road it is on and any other notes relating to the point.

THE KNOWLEDGE

Example:
London Coliseum
St Martins Lane, ES, one-way SB. LOL only, F/L William IV St

(ES = East Side, SB = Southbound)

As you become increasingly fluent with your points your recalling time will decrease. The app I used had a schedule where it would show a new card within the hour, then the next day, then two days, four days and so on. If you lose fluency it moves back up the pile, which makes the card appear more frequently again.

I have heard of some students who never actively revise points. Having seen it and driven the turnaround, they were able to easily recall it, but I found the whole process of writing out my flashcards using the Anki app and then recalling them cemented the points in my mind.

The quest for pointing is endless. You cannot learn every single point in London but you can do yourself a favour and learn as many as possible. How many you end up with depends on how long you are on The Knowledge and your intensity. When I got the golden handshake, I had accumulated approximately 9,000 points, while my friend and call over partner had 15,000! It is not the defining factor of your success but it will certainly help you along the way and in the cab!

BIKE LISTS

Before physically going out pointing, it is wise to generate a bike list. This is a list of points you aim to find when you next go out in your car or on your bike and will ensure that you are not roaming the streets endlessly. It is recommended that you collect 20-30 points in a session, as you will often pick up more than you have on your list. I would personally give myself a maximum of four hours pointing time (not including my commute), as there's only so much your brain can take in and its useful to have a rough time scale so that you can schedule when you start/leave.

Whenever I dropped a point on the daily sheet, I would make a note of it and what postcode it resided in. Over time, some postcodes would be more prominent than others. Let's just say, I built up 15 points in SE10, I would then make it my priority to visit that area next. Be smart with your time; visit points in postcodes that are in neighbouring areas to the one you are visiting, and plan a route across the map. For instance, I would come into London via the A12, visit a few points in E3, then go through the Blackwall Tunnel, visit my SE10 points, add in a few points from SE5, come back through the Rotherhithe tunnel, find a few more points in E2, before jumping back on the A12 and heading home.

Recap

- A point is a point of interest in London
- A point of interest can be absolutely anything within the six-mile radius of Charing Cross
- To learn a point fully, you not only need to know which street/road it occupies, but also how to set and leave it from any direction/with restriction

POINT TO POINT

Point to Point (P2P) is essentially the crux of The Knowledge. It is where you begin to combine your Blue Books with your obtained points to start formulating your own routes across London.

It is the process of being asked one random point and a second random point. Once you have identified both points (by naming the correct street/road they occupy) you are then expected to be able to orally call the most direct and legal route between the two. Naming every street/road on the route and calling the correct direction onto each road.

P2P is best started once you have completed your Blue Book runs and obtained around 1,000 points. It can be started earlier but if you haven't completed your Blue Books there may be missing roads that could prove useful in helping you to formulate your routes.

P2P is very daunting and arguably one of the toughest hurdles in The Knowledge. It is when you convert your learnt routes into unique routes, which are thought of on the spot once your two points have been given to you. It is exactly what you are required to do in an appearance (examination) situation and is the thought simulation that is most similar to really driving a cab.

POINT TO POINT

One of the best ways of easing yourself into P2P is to use Blue Book runs but slightly vary the start and end point. So, in the example of Manor House Station to Gibson Square, you could change the points to The Happy Man PH (Public House - Pub) to the Business Design Centre instead. The majority of the run remains the same but you may have to add a few extra roads at the start and the end.

As you are calling your run, your call-over partner will be penning the run on the map. Once you have finished calling, look at your "line" and check with your "cotton" (piece of string) to see if it is as straight and direct as possible. When you start P2P, you may find that your lines are all over the place and you call a few "bananas" (bent lines not straight). I know I did this plenty of times, even at the later stages of The Knowledge!

Congratulations, you have just called your first ever P2P run! You will do this many, many more times on your Knowledge journey.

Most students subscribe to daily "sheets". These are collected by point collectors outside of The Knowledge exam centre, categorised by stage (i.e. 56's, 28's, 21's) and arranged in order of the examiner. A daily routine on The Knowledge (once you are at P2P level) is to complete a sheet at your relevant stage and a succeeding stage if you are close to it.

For example, it is very wise to do P2P for at least three months prior to your first appearance. So for the three months preceding my first 56 appearance (and before the map test), I ensured I did as many of the 56 level questions as I could. These sheets are like mock exam papers. Yes, they have actually been asked in an appearance but that doesn't mean you are likely to get the same question or point again.

Remember that an examiner can ask you about any destination or route within the six-mile radius of London!

Just get them there

The most important tip with P2P – from the beginning right until the final run you call in an exam – is to **get them there**. If you can't think of a suitable line or see one, just get the examiner there, however possible. If you cannot answer the question/complete the route you will be scored a 0. If, however, you get them there you will get a score. Yes, the line might be a shocking banana, but you could still score a two, a three, or it might not be that bad and you will get a six!

This is often a good simulation of driving the cab. You might hit roadworks and have to change your direction, but you wouldn't dream of stopping the cab and saying, "Sorry sir, you'll have to walk from here." Your job is to get the passenger to their intended destination.

I would always complete the run fully with my call-over partners. If you miscall a road and start heading in the wrong direction, don't restart, carry on and try so that you can get back on course and complete the run. In the real exam chair, you are not allowed to recall your run.

In my very first appearance, I went off track and went wide. I could have said, "Sorry ma'am, I've gone wide," or do as I did and continue the route. I scored a six for that particular run but overall, it was enough to score the appearance!

When practising P2P with a partner, check your line after calling. If the line is bad, look at it have a think about a more ideal route. Rub off the line and then recall it again. Remember, you learn from your mistakes and bad lines.

POINT TO POINT

Daily sheets are only a guide to what has been asked in an appearance. Sometimes, some students don't give in their runs. This means there are many more questions that the examiner could have asked. Students also naturally forget runs and points (believe me, I would find it hard to recall my name or the day of the week after an appearance!). The sheets are a great starting point because of this but don't forget to challenge yourself beyond the sheet.

Break the run down or start from the end

It can be incredibly daunting to think about all of the roads required to get from one side of the map to the other, especially on long runs.

One strategy is to break the run in half. When going from Whitechapel station to Latimer Road station, try and visualise the mid-point of the run. I would probably aim for Oxford Circus. Part 1: Whitechapel station to Oxford Circus, Part 2: Oxford Circus to Latimer Road station. This method would help me call straighter lines and assemble the run quicker.

Some find it helpful to work the run backwards. So to finish at Latimer Road station, I know I probably need to get to Ladbroke Grove, and to get to Ladbroke Grove I need to get to Bayswater, and so on. I use this tactic when driving in the cab a lot. Thinking about how you have to set the final point can really influence how you build your line.

Learn some stock calls and cut down on your thinking time

THE KNOWLEDGE

As you get more advanced with point to point, it is worth learning set routes or set ways of calling from one area of the map to another. This is very beneficial on long routes as it drastically cuts down on your thinking time.

It is worth noting down the kind of lines and patterns you regularly see in your P2P and creating multiple stock calls.

Let's say St Mary's Hospital to Lavender Hill Police Station. A quick think or look at the map will tell you that you need to go through Hyde Park and down to Albert Bridge to line up with Latchmere Road and then the police station. I would always spend far too long thinking about how to get from Hyde Park to Albert Bridge. Rather than working out the optimum route every time, I learnt a stock call which always used the same roads. There's a huge option of roads and streets that you can call, but if you commit to learning one set, it makes the whole route a lot easier to think about.

My stock call from Hyde Park to Albert Bridge was:

WCD, F Alexandra Gate, F Exhibition Road, R Thurloe Place, L Cromwell Place, F and B/L Onslow Square, F Sydney Place, R Fulham Road, L Sydney Street, R Kings Road, L Oakley Street, F Albert Bridge.

Football runs are also a good example of this, as they use large points and direct roads to get yourself across the map efficiently. For example; Chelsea FC to Arsenal FC. If an examiner gave you Chelsea Pensioner PH to Nags Head Shopping Centre, your pre-work learning football runs would have given you 95% of the route, so all you need to do is think about the leave and set.

Even on a longer route, such as Putney Library to Woodberry Down Estate, you know this line pretty much runs through Chelsea FC to Arsenal FC and beyond once

55

you start being able to visualise the map. This cuts down about 70% of the thinking for the run.

The compass course taught at Knowledge Point school was a valuable resource for streamlining my calling in this way.

Recap

- Point to point is the process of orally calling from one point of interest to another
- You are expected to be fluent, clear and confident in your P2P calling
- P2P is one of the most difficult stages of The Knowledge
- We are aiming for the most direct line, but fear not if you call a banana. It is just as important, if not more, to call the line with confidence and, above all, finish calling the route.

CALL-OVER PARTNER

A call-over partner (COP) is a valuable tool on your Knowledge journey. Yes, The Knowledge can be done without a COP, but you could make a lot more mistakes as a result and take much longer to complete the process. Most knowledge boys and girls look for a call-over partner once they start point to point, but they can be a valuable asset from the beginning of your knowledge journey.

Remember a COP is someone to call over runs with, either at home, in front of the map or at a Knowledge school (coffee and biscuits optional). Some other chat might come up, but largely the session is about calling runs of London together. A COP that restricts this important task isn't worth having.

I've outlined several benefits to having a COP below:

Accountability - Like a gym partner, if you arrange to call over with your COP you are more likely to stick to it as you are accountable to each other.

Competition/Inspiration - Seeing your COP succeed through scoring or even getting their badge can be a huge motivational boost and competition setter.

CALL-OVER PARTNER

Penning your lines - Your COP will have a good knowledge of the roads and streets and so will be able to pen your lines as quickly as you can call them.

Fault finding - Everyone's Knowledge journey is different. You might glance over a mistake that your COP finds obvious and vice versa. There's plenty of illegal manoeuvres that I would not have known about had it not been for my COPs.

The best COPs are those who are actually doing The Knowledge and have a good work ethic. You might know a cabbie who you can call over with, but remember that their Knowledge is not as strong as a Knowledge student. Cabbies often have their set ways of driving which would not satisfy the best line penned up on the map, and so would be more lenient about looking at a slightly curved line. A good COP will challenge you on your lines, and often look at alternatives to improve them.

DO

A good COP will be roughly at the same level as you on The Knowledge, but don't rule out anyone who is at a higher or lower level. We all learn at a different pace and in different ways, so your COP may be able to provide an essential nugget of information that you hadn't ever considered at your level.

Get as many COPs as you can. The more heads you can converse with, the more routes/roads/points you can pick up, the more you will be multiplying your best chances of success.

Set your level of expectation by making it clear to your COP if you're going to call over for two hours or you have to shoot off early. Are you going to call one run at a time and check immediately afterwards, or do four runs exam style then check the runs?

DON'T

Use friends or family - Your COP must be studying The Knowledge. You might get your spouse, friends or family to help you out but they will lack The Knowledge to correct your mistakes. They won't be able to pen your runs as quickly as you can call them and won't generally be as interested in the process (believe me, it is incredibly boring as an outsider).

Criticise their lines - We all have our own strengths and weaknesses. Sometimes, after a long day of studying, the line isn't so obvious. Pen the line-up and let your COP criticise their own lines. I was very pessimistic and critical of my own lines, I always wanted to improve myself, even if the line was perfectly adequate. Conversely, some people like to achieve the minimum and use the most basic roads.

CALL-OVER PARTNER

MAP TEST

The Map Test is to The Knowledge what the theory test is to your driving test. It is an examination taken prior to appearances that aims to ensure you are ready to progress onto the oral examination stage.

Fundamentally, the map test is a multiple choice examination paper. However, you are required to have completed all 320 Blue Book runs and amassed a good knowledge of points (around 2,000-3,000) before sitting the exam.

The Map test is split into two parts; Blue Book Runs and Points. Both sections are weighted 50% each. The best score available is 100. The pass mark is 70 (70%).

Blue Book Runs

In the first half of the map test, you are given five Blue Book runs. Each one has three possible answers. The objective of these questions is to determine the most direct and legal route of the Blue Book run given.

Usually, one line will be correct within the choice of three answers, one line will run wide, and the final run will contain an illegal. Your extensive Knowledge of the Blue Book and the map should be able to direct you to the correct

MAP TEST

answer. Please note that Blue Book runs are interpretations, so you may find that the correct answer in the exam does not abide by the run that was described by Knowledge Point or WizAnn. Both schools create their own runs, neither one is more correct than the other, just as driving a route in the cab can generate multiple options. So be wary as the exam paper may not have the exact same route as you learnt on the Blue Book!

Each correct run will score you 10 marks, meaning that five correct answers will score you the maximum of 50 marks for this section.

Points

The second half of the map test consists of 25 questions. Each question is delivered in the form of a point, such as: Where is The Islington Ecology Centre located? Each question has six potential answers. You must choose one answer by giving the street/road you believe the point is located on.

Each correct answer will score you two marks, meaning that 25 correct answers will score you the maximum of 50 marks for this section.

Your map tests results are emailed to you that afternoon or the day after your exam. You will receive a subsequent letter outlining the next steps. This will depend on your result, i.e. when your first appearance will be if you have passed or when you can next resit if you have not.

APPEARANCES

WHAT IS AN APPEARANCE?

Appearances are the gruelling oral examinations that all aspiring cab drivers must sit (usually a minimum of 12) to earn their badge and the right to work as a cab driver.

Once you have passed your written map test (Stage 2), you are invited to sit your first oral appearance (Stage 3, also known as 56's). This usually comes within a month of passing your map test.

Appearances are conducted face to face (hence the term appearance). The examiner is sat behind a desk with a map in front of them to assess the examination, while you, as the candidate, sit directly opposite. You will have no aids or material (only your memory) to assist in the examination.

An appearance usually consists of just four P2P questions. Each question is performed sequentially. Once a start and end point have been identified by the candidate, they then must orally recite the most direct and legal route between the two points of interest. Examiners can ask any point within The Knowledge's six-mile radius.

APPEARANCES

Below is an example of four questions I was asked from various appearances.

- Park Plaza City Hotel - Churchill Hyatt Hotel
- Hospital of St John & Elizabeth - The RAFT
- Battersea Cats and Dogs Home - The Dog's Trust
- Willesden Junction Station - Rosslyn Park Football Club

Once you have completed all four questions, the examiner will let you know if you have scored or if you have not been so successful. I will break down the scoring system in the next section.

APPEARANCE SCORING SYSTEM

What determines my grade in an appearance?

The most commonly awarded grades are either C or D. Here is a breakdown of the grade criteria in a single appearance.

0-23 D
24-32 C
32-36 B
37-40 A

A perfect appearance would score 40 points (A). I am now going to outline how the points are awarded.

Each appearance contains four questions. A maximum score of 10 points can be awarded for each question (4 x 10 = 40).

At the start of each question you begin with the 10 points, and then points are deducted for the following:

- Not knowing the point of interest (POI) - Deduct 1 point per POI not known (also known as "dropping a point")
- Hesitancy
- Not taking the most direct route available
- Illegal manoeuvre (doing a turn when it is not permitted by road signage, a U-turn, calling the wrong way down a one-way street, etc.) - deduct 10 points
- Calling the wrong road/forgetting a road - deduct one point

Here is an example:

1st Question

2 POIs dropped (2 points deducted)
Line slightly wide (1 point deducted)
Called fluently, no illegals and all the road names correct (0 points deducted)
Maximum 10, minus 3 points
Examiner Score = **7**

2nd Question

No POIs Dropped (0 points deducted)
Line perfect (0 points deducted)
Hesitant in calling roads (2 points deducted)
Some roads forgotten (2 points deducted)
Maximum 10, minus 4 points
Examiner Score = **6**

3rd Question
No POIs Dropped (0 points deducted)
Perfect Line (0 points deducted)
Called fluently, correct road names (0 points deducted)
Called an illegal manoeuvre (10 points deducted)
Maximum 10, minus 10 points
Examiner Score = **0**

4th Question
No POIs dropped (0 points deducted)
Perfect Line (0 pointed deducted)
Called fluently, no illegals and all the road names correct (0 pointers deducted)
Maximum 10, minus 0 points
Examiner Score = **10**

Total Score (7+6+0+10) = 23 (D)

You are only made aware of the score at the end of the appearance. Not knowing if you have done an illegal on any of your runs increases the tension even more. As the exams are exceptionally difficult, most Knowledge boys and girls only care about getting a pass, so a C is the standard they aim for.

In the example outlined above, it shows how just one mistake, an illegal manoeuvre, cost the entire appearance (let's just say it was calling a right turn when a right turn is banned).

Think of the appearance like a dance or gymnastics routine that is being judged. A gymnast might take a risk, such as an intricate backflip, to try and impress the judges and get a high score; however, they might not be able to land this manoeuvre, which would shatter their performance and result in a lower score than if they had played safe and completed a smooth routine. The same applies to The Knowledge. Having good knowledge, showing confidence and being fluent is generally a better option than risking a route or road restriction that you aren't familiar with.

Progressing through stages

The appearance scoring system determines how quickly you progress through the various stages of appearances. It can be complicated to understand but I have broken it down into the various stages:

Stage 3 - 56's (Average of 56 days/two months between each exam)
Stage 4 - 28's (Average of 28 days/one month between each exam)
Stage 5 - 21's (Average of 21 days/three weeks between each exam)

So, as you advance through the stages and your grasp of the Knowledge increases, the time between each exam becomes shorter and you are required to attend more regularly. The later stages of the appearances generally increase in difficulty as your knowledge of London grows. For instance, 56's appearances may be centred around large points of interest, such as train stations, hotels, or restaurants. 28's appearances can become more obscure and for 21's you are expected to learn topographical knowledge, such as what is showing at each theatre or to name establishments with a rooftop bar.

To progress from one stage to the next, you need to acquire at least 12 points across a series of exams with the following grading criteria:

APPEARANCES

D - 0 Points
C - 3 Points
B - 4 Points
A - 6 Points

So, using the example of Stage 3 (56's), here is how a stage may pan out.

Exam date	Grade	Points this exam	Running total
16th Nov	C	3	3
5th Jan	D	0	3
3rd Mar	D	0	3
6th May	C	3	6
8th July	B	4	10
5th Sep	C	3	13
Drop to 28's			

In this example, it has taken the candidate 11 months to acquire the minimum points (12) to progress onto the next stage.

However, if a candidate accumulates a total of four D's on any one stage, they are taken back to the start of that stage (red lined), as shown below.

68

THE KNOWLEDGE

Exam date	Grade	Points this exam	Running total
16th Nov	C	3	3
5th Jan	D	0	3
3rd Mar	D	0	3
6th May	C	3	6
8th July	B	4	10
5th Sep	D	0	10
8th Nov	D (4th D)	0	10
Redlined to beginning of 56's			

This can be very grueling as the candidate had scored three times in total on the 8th of July, and therefore only needed one more C to achieve their "drop" to the next stage 28's.

It is an example like this in the examination process that can add an extra year onto the entire process.

If the candidate gets redlined twice on the same stage, i.e. 56's redline, they are pushed back to the previous stage! In this case, the previous stage would be the map test! This is where it pays dividends to study The Knowledge as frequently as possible.

69

APPEARANCES

I've outlined a Knowledge journey below.

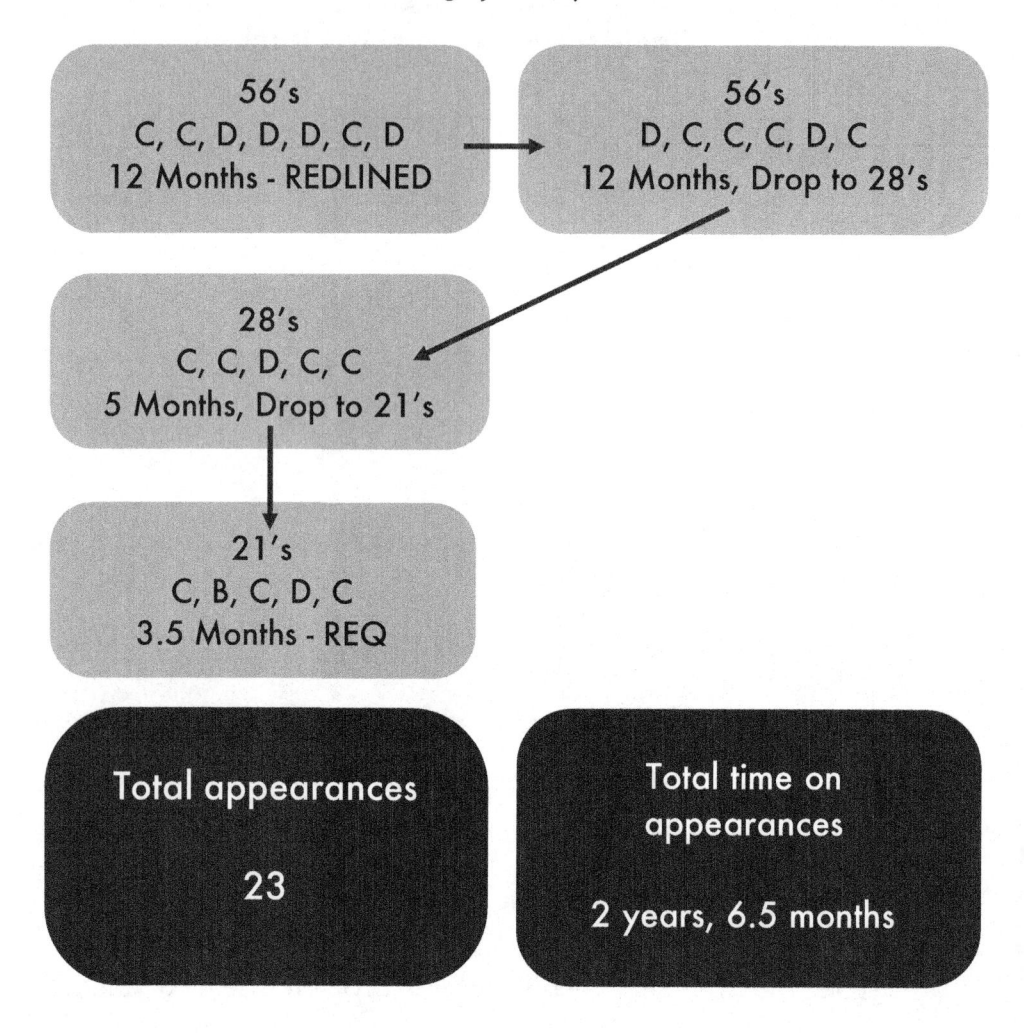

56's
C, C, D, D, D, C, D
12 Months - REDLINED

→

56's
D, C, C, C, D, C
12 Months, Drop to 28's

28's
C, C, D, C, C
5 Months, Drop to 21's

21's
C, B, C, D, C
3.5 Months - REQ

Total appearances

23

Total time on appearances

2 years, 6.5 months

THE KNOWLEDGE

WHAT DO I WEAR TO AN APPEARANCE?

Anytime you visit the TfL Taxi and Private Hire Office (230 Blackfriars Road, but the door is on Chancel Street), you are expected to "wear suitable attire that reflects well on the profession". This is also expected on your map test. I wore a full suit at my voluntary assessment. The examiner commented on some of the more casually dressed candidates and recommended that they should be in more suitable attire the next time they came to the PCO.

They are called appearances because you physically appear at the examination centre. As part of this, you are expected to wear a full suit, tie and smart shoes. This is the accepted tradition and it is looked down upon if you deviate from this in any way (a lack of a suit is accepted with female candidates; in this instance, treat the appearance attire like a formal job interview). Even at your voluntary assessment or map test, it is your ultimate chance to shine and show your calibre as a person, not just as a student.

The Knowledge is as much a character building exercise as it is a formal examination process. There have been rumours of gentlemen being sent home for not wearing a tie. An appearance is about you conveying your Knowledge of London in the calmest and professional manner possible; therefore, your attire should reflect all of those qualities.

I would always make sure I was freshly showered, hair cut the day before, shoes polished and suit pressed. I placed my appearance card in a special wallet to ensure it did not crease or bend. During your time on The Knowledge you will be seen by multiple examiners. If you regularly turn up late, with your hair scruffy and card folded in half, what image do you think this will project to the examiner? They will have every reason to doubt your ability and whether you have even put the effort into studying.

HOW DO I CONDUCT MYSELF IN AN APPEARANCE?

An appearance is what I imagine it's like going for a parole hearing.

On your very first appearance, the examiner will go over the examination process, do's and don'ts and what you can expect going forward.

Here are the main rules:

- Answer the examiner as sir or ma'am
- Don't shake their hand
- Don't question their judgement

My rule was never to assume anything. As soon as your name is called you follow the examiner into their room. They usually hold the door, ask for your scorecard and instruct you to sit down. I had one examiner who took my card but didn't instruct me to sit down. I didn't want to assume that I could so I asked the question, "Sir, may I be seated?" to which he replied, "Of course, unless you wish to conduct the appearance standing up?"

Some examiners will do their best to settle your nerves. Having one examiner for a second time (he had previously scored me a D), he looked at my scorecard whilst I took my seat and said, "Well, looks like I'm not on your Christmas card list, Mr. Hutley." Other examiners are very brief and to the point. I've had appearances where the first question was asked before I'd even had a chance to sit down!

Not shaking their hand seems very odd as many people would liken the experience to a job interview. Just think of it like *The Apprentice*. No candidate shakes Alan Sugar's hand until they actually get the job. The Knowledge is exactly the same, the handshake is reserved until the magical day when you achieve your Req (requisition to become a cab driver).

At the end of the appearance, most examiners will let you know if you have scored or not. This is down to the examiner, some will return your scorecard and merely say, "See you again in X amount of days." Depending on the outcome, I would gladly take my card, thank the examiner for their time and wish them a good day as I left.

PREPARING YOUR MIND STATE

I took all 13 of my appearances with the most serious consideration. Preparing like an athlete, I left no stone unturned in my search for an advantage that I could give myself in the appearance room. These were my preparation techniques. I'm not prescribing these, as we all work differently, but these may give you some inspiration in how to get the most from your appearances.

7 DAYS PRIOR TO EXAM

APPERANCES

Develop a good sleep routine by going to bed at the same time and waking at the same time. Doing late night/early morning pointing can really wreak havoc on your sleeping patterns. Your body is a machine, it needs as much sleep as possible to repair the cells in your body and, more importantly for appearances, in your brain. It is also linked to creating a stronger memory and greater retention in those who are studying.

Start cutting out caffeine. There are lots of studies which show that caffeine can have anxiety-producing effects. Traces of caffeine can be present in the body for up to a week after consumption. As anxiety and exams really don't go together, I didn't want to take the chance that this would have any effect on my performance. Remember, caffeine has a half-life of five hours, so if you have a strong coffee at 3pm, chances are that your body will still be processing almost half of that drink by the time you go to bed. Again, I didn't want the possibility of anything disrupting good quality sleep.

I would also cut out alcohol in the week prior for the same reasons. Don't worry if you are a drinker, you can treat yourself to your favourite once you have scored!

Drink plenty of water. Your brain is an organ, so it needs the best fuel and resources to do its job properly. It needs a lot of water to operate at the desired level on The Knowledge. Drink a lot in the days leading up to an exam, and also on the day itself.

NIGHT BEFORE THE EXAM

THE KNOWLEDGE

Try and complete all the runs from your level on the sheet. So if you are currently on 56's just focus on that level. Also, look at what the examiners have asked on other stages. Don't worry about calling the other levels, just look at the type of runs and type of points asked. Do this on the day of the exam. I actually had a question that an examiner had asked the previous day once.

After studying that evening, I would go for a short cycle ride; nothing intensive, just a nice leisurely cycle that would raise my heart rate and get me out of the house. I found this helped with my nerves into the evening. There are plenty of studies online which show that exercise is linked with better memory retention.

DAY OF THE EXAM

Get to the test centre early

Quite an obvious tip, but you're more likely to become stressed if you get caught in traffic, and that emotion can spill over into your exam time. Don't go into The Public Carriage Office until your required time (usually 20 minutes before the time that's stated on your card).

Go for a walk

A brisk walk is good to help wake up the brain. You can take in a few points and walk a few tricky streets. Many students are asked points that are in proximity to the PCO. My call-over partner was asked The English Touring Theatre on Short Street SE1; a point I had only found while walking prior to my examination. During my final exam, I was asked Nelson Square, again another point that's incredibly close to The Public Carriage Office.

Have a banana

Studies show that bananas contain natural ingredients that have an anxiety-reducing effect. I would eat one on the final walk up to the PCO.

Listen to music

Professional athletes do this as part of their routine before competing and we, as Knowledge students, are arguably no different. I would have a single playlist (I made one for each stage: 56's, 28's, 21's etc.) that I would play whilst walking around SE1 in preparation for my appearance.

Breathing

It is only natural for your heart rate to accelerate whilst you are sat in the ring of fire (the seats directly outside the appearance rooms) awaiting to hear your name being called by an examiner. If your heart rate accelerates your body will have to work harder to distribute blood and oxygen to the important areas of your body. In this case, your brain! If you focus on rhythmic breathing (not deep breathing), you will be able to better regulate your heart rate and the quality of the oxygen that's distributed in your body.

Don't overthink

I remember seeing some students in the waiting area studying their A-Z. One guy even asked me whether a right turn was banned at a certain junction. At this point in the game, all the hard work has been done and no amount of thought is going to make the exam easier; there is nothing more you can do. In fact, it is a complete waste of your energy and resources to think about routes and points that you are statistically unlikely to be asked. Just accept that you can get any examiner, and they can ask you just about anything. Deal with the punches once they start coming your way.

"EVERYONE HAS A PLAN UNTIL THEY GET PUNCHED IN THE MOUTH." MIKE TYSON

Habit and routine is a powerful machine. By using all of these techniques you are giving your mind the best chance of success. It is good to mentally tick each of these operations off one by one as you complete them, providing a nice confirmation bias for your mind, as you are psychologically winning every task. Your appearance is then just another small task to complete.

WHAT DO EXAMINERS ASK DURING APPEARANCES?

During most appearances, examiners will generally ask you a point of interest or a physical road/street. While there is no official ruling, you are generally asked larger/more popular points on 56's. On the stage 28's, points become obscurer and even more so on 21's.

Whilst we'd like to think that examiners will be lenient on 56's, we can't assume anything on The Knowledge. I have heard of students going for their very first appearance and the examiner giving points of interest that even a student on 21's might struggle with. All you can do is keep on working, keep on taking in new points and come back and try again.

As you progress through the stages, your knowledge of points should expand, as well as your topographical knowledge. For 21's, you should prepare for the examiners to ask you questions such as "What theatre is The Lion King shown at?" At this crucial stage, you need to demonstrate that you know London on a molecular level. Cabbies that knew I was on The Knowledge updated me if a new point came about, or a temporary exhibit was installed. Examiners are also cab drivers, so they will test you on these obscurities to find out how hard you are working.

TOP APPEARANCE TIPS

Keep it calm, fluent and legal

I spent a lot of time studying but even if you somehow studied The Knowledge 24/7, the examiner could ask a point of interest that you did not know.

So I accepted that yes, I might drop POI's, as this was something I *could not* control, but nerves and illegal manoeuvres (to some degree) were within my control.

Yes, I did once call an illegal in an appearance and scored exactly 23 points. A big fat D which resulted in me having an extra 56 days on my Knowledge journey.

On a later appearance, I was asked to call from Embankment Gardens to Smith Terrace without using Royal Hospital Road. I knew that I could somehow get to Smith Terrace using Tite Street, but I was not confident about the exact lefts and rights around Tedworth Sq, and how Smith Terrace sat in conjunction with this. So, to be safe, I called all along Chelsea Embankment, up Chelsea Bridge Rd into St Leonards Terrace via Lower Sloane St, L Turks Row, R Franklins etc.

To cut a long story short, I knew that trying to guess my way up Tite Street and around Tedworth Square was likely to score me a 0. Going the long way round wasn't ideal, but it still scored me a 6! This was very fortunate as my total score for the whole appearance was 29, a pass with a C! Had I taken the risk my score could have been 23 (D), and I wasn't prepared to lose the appearance and 28 days of my life!

Give yourself some thinking time, but don't take too long

Don't make the mistake of rushing off before you've thought your run through. Some lines will come to you instantly, but it will take a lot more strenuous thought to assemble others in your mind.

Even if the line is very apparent and you feel you are ready to call, double-check it in your head. There is no prize or bonus for being able to answer the question as quickly as possible, so take your time here.

Whilst there is no set rule, most examiners will give you between 30-60 seconds thinking time. When you are doing P2P at home, I would urge you to try and start calling at 30 seconds or maybe even 20 seconds. This is a good way of toughening yourself up for the exam room.

I remember being given a very difficult run by a formidable examiner. It was my last run of the appearance and I felt like I had been thinking for nearly two minutes and still couldn't produce a line in my head.

"Mr. Hutley, I'd like you to start calling the run now," the examiner said.

The appearance room is probably the most intense place on earth for any Knowledge student. When you throw in the examiner's command and the fact I had to start calling a run without the faintest clue where I might end up, it was probably one of the most disempowering experiences of my life.

I believe the runs prior to this must have satisfied the examiner. I had stumbled my way into a difficult gyratory of roads and my calling had noticeably slowed to a pause.

"Well, there's only one way out now, keep going," the examiner said.

I slowly released the roads from my mind's grasp, as though one incorrect name here would set off an audible siren that would end the entire appearance.

"Right Kenworthy Road."

"Yes," the examiner affirmed

"Left Wick Road."

"Yes."

"Right East Cross Route."

I'm pleased to say that after this ordeal – during which the final run felt like an entire appearance in itself – the examiner scored me and gave me my drop onto 28's.

HESITATION KILLS

Have you ever had an experience with a smooth and knowledgeable salesperson? Remember how effortless and flawless their delivery was when they sold you a car or TV? Conversely, you may be able to remember a salesperson who demonstrated the opposite traits. Maybe they mumbled and hesitated or just crumbled under the questions you asked them? Both salespeople probably had the same product knowledge, but it's no surprise that one shines far greater than the other.

Your appearance is exactly the same. You need to deliver with conviction your outstanding Knowledge of London in the smoothest way possible.

During my first experience of doing P2P, a call-over partner at The London Knowledge school in Grays showed me a small tally chart of six strikes after calling a run.

"Do you know what that is?" he asked. "That's how many time you said the word 'Urrr' when calling that run."

Technically, that could be six points off of a run, quite a dramatic drop in a score!

Examiners can't see inside your head. I have had appearances where I have been bricking it, calling a route through a part of London that I may be "weaker" on. So long as you exude confidence and the line is legal, the examiner can only score you. We all have our weaknesses but to display any hesitancy shows this to the examiner. Be the flawless salesperson, sell your knowledge in the most convincing and enjoyable manner possible, with confidence!

POINT COLLECTORS

Outside of the test centre, you will notice a couple of individuals with a clipboard or iPad. These are point collectors. They are also Knowledge students who collect runs that have been given to candidates in an appearance and can then be assembled into a daily appearance sheet (provided by schools for a minimal subscription).

The data you provide is essential for every student on The Knowledge, as the more people who give their runs in, the better the picture will be of what is being asked at the examination centre. It usually takes one to two minutes to give the collectors your runs and then you can head home.

I never understood those who didn't give in their runs to the point collectors. It would often be those who walked off in frustration after getting a D. But this will achieve nothing collectively for The Knowledge world.

Whenever I didn't score, I found the point collectors helped to lift my spirits, and whenever I did score, they made it feel even better.

After an appearance, you are given a sheet of paper from the examiner that shows exactly how your score is constructed (how many points were dropped, called wide etc.). When I left the exam room, I would sit in the main reception area and recall the questions and points I was asked while they were still fresh and write these on the back of the sheet of paper. I would urge everyone to do this before going outside and seeing the point collectors, as it makes the system a lot more efficient. Sitting alone will also allow a much better recall of your appearance before you step outside and are distracted by the world.

BETWEEN APPEARANCES

I would vary my schedule depending on the amount of time leading up to an appearance.

For instance, I found the best time to go and learn lots of new points would be in the days/week immediately after your most recent appearance. This is because it allows them plenty of time to sink in for the next appearance one month/two months later. Conversely, you wouldn't want to do an intensive pointing session the day before your next appearance. It's practically pointless (pun intended) as you have little time to commit them to memory.

In the week/days that precede an appearance, I would focus on exercises that enable me to call more fluently and remember road names, such as calling Blue Books or road streams. Road streaming is almost comparable to the vocal warm-ups that speakers or television presenters do. The

APPERANCES

objective is to call roads in one direction for as long and fluently as possible, ideally from one side of the map to the other.

Example

F High Rd Tottenham, F Stamford Hill, L Northwold Rd, F Rectory Rd, R Manse Rd, F Evering Rd, L Stoke Newington Rd, F Kingsland High St, F Kingsland Rd, F Shoreditch High St, F Norton Folgate, F Bishopsgate... etc. etc.

Call as far as you go and then turnaround and come back. These exercises are important as sometimes you need to call a long sequence of roads in an appearance so this practice gets you adapted to calling for a long, continuous period of time, and mean you will not get caught out by the one-way systems that work one way but not the other. (Northworld and Rectory is only southbound, northbound is just Stoke Newington High St).

Effective scheduling between 21's can be really tricky. With just three weeks between each appearance, it feels like you are back at home in bed one moment and then back at the PCO the next day for another appearance. Do what is right for you and your schedule. By this point, you should be self-critical and know where your strengths and weaknesses lie. When I got to 21's I revised the roads and squares as I noticed these were being asked a lot. I was absolutely fine with physical points (restaurants, hotels, etc), but a plain road I would drop, even though I had driven down it hundreds of times

LEARN FROM YOUR FAILURES

While there is no feeling quite like obtaining a score on The Knowledge (it's a euphoria that usually lasts an evening, before you return to a solid Knowledge schedule the next morning), it can often be a relief just to walk away from the PCO with a D as the tension that has been building up for two months or so has just deflated. Now is a good time to analyse your performance. There may be several factors that contribute to this, and the examiner may even go over them with you. Alternatively, your score sheet should be able to highlight your weaknesses.

Too many points dropped - Put more effort into revising and collecting points.

Too much hesitation - Focus on your confidence and practice calling more fluently. Ask your call-over partner to put you under a bit of pressure (limit your run generation thinking time and get them to call a few random roads whilst you are calling as a way of overcoming distraction).

Roads not called correctly - Do more Blue Book calling or fluency exercises.

Line too wide - Spend more time doing point to point, ensuring that you pen up your runs every time to allow your mental map to build.

Too many illegals - Check your runs more often, don't call a route if you are not 100% confident of its legality.

Even after a successful score, I still critiqued my appearance as, ultimately, you will have a weakness at every appearance. Some believe that your strengths and weaknesses go on your file and can be used to tailor your next appearances. During my appearance where I achieved my drop from 56's to 28's, the examiner asked me lots of obscure points in E3. This was my last run of the appearance and, thankfully, he was lenient with me and eventually gave me an easier point. I scraped through with a C. So the next day I went to the area he tested me on and learnt as much as I could.

While giving in my runs to the point collectors, I would hear on the odd occasion an obnoxious Knowledge student, say: "Oh, such and such examiner wanted to give me a D." Or "Their points were ridiculous," etc etc. It always seemed appropriate that the students with this attitude somehow ended up with a D.

Examiners are not there to intentionally give hard-working students a D. London Taxi driver numbers are slowly diminishing, and the fewer drivers, the less reliable service we can offer. Therefore, examiners *want you to score*. That's right, I firmly believe that every examiner wants students to score. However, examiners are also responsible for upholding the impeccable standard that every aspiring cab driver must reach; thus, they will only score those who have put the work in and can demonstrate it. By knowing obscure points, navigating difficult roads and calling with fluency, you are demonstrating to the examiner how hard you have been working in this process!

GETTING YOUR REQ

This is the magical day we all crave for on The Knowledge. Your "Req" is your "Requisition to become a cab driver". To put it another way, this is when you have reached the required standard to be a London cab driver. You get the golden handshake and have completed The Knowledge.

This is awarded on the 21's stage once you have achieved 12 Points (4 consecutive C's or equivalent grades) at that level. You could be 3-0 up (3 C's in a row), so all you need is one more score, but be careful here, your faultless score at this stage doesn't guarantee any form of success and it is ultimately just another appearance. Some examiners are known to engineer it so that the final run is the same as the first Blue Book run, "Manor House Station to Gibson Square", a touching way to end your Knowledge journey. For other examiners, it is business as usual.

For my req, I had a personalised appearance, a trademark of a particular examiner. This used points of interest related to areas of my life.

Upon seeing the examiner and being beckoned into the appearance room, I prompted this tactic, and so ensured that all my answers to the examiner would be directed to points that I know. The questions then started flowing.

"What have you done prior to The Knowledge, Mr. Hutley?"

"I studied Film & TV at university, sir."

"Okay then, sir, let's see what your knowledge of film and TV studios is like."

I'd fallen for the trap, other than the obvious ITV or BBC HQs, I was completely clueless here. The examiner then continued to batter me with what felt like a barrage of points. "No, sir," "I can't see it, Sir," "Sorry, sir," I said, running out of ways to say no.

"Cherry Duck Studios?"

My mind cast back to over a year earlier when I was sat in Derek O'Reilly's "Compass Course" at Knowledge Point school on Brewery Road. I remembered him casually saying

"Cherry Duck Studios", and like the eager student I was, I jotted the point down as one to go and visit. I'm very glad I did!

"Sampson Street, sir!"

"Okay, and we are going to go to Bow River Village."

Recollecting the experience, I assumed this point was asked due to its proximity to the Three Mills Studios, near to the Bow interchange.

"Blackwall Tunnel northern approach, sir!"

I carefully constructed the run in my mind, not entirely sure the best way to leave Wapping (Wapping Wall, Garnet Street and Glamis Road still confuse me to this day). Slowly and deliberately, I orally delivered the run to the examiner, ensuring not to hesitate, which could have subtracted even more points.

"LOR Sampson St, L Vaughan Way, R The Highway, L Butcher Row, R Commercial Rd, L Yorkshire Rd, R Salmon Lane, F Rhodeswell Rd, B/R Turners Rd, R St Pauls Way, F Devons Rd, L Blackwall Tunnel Northern approach, B/L Bow Interchange slip rd, Comply Bow Interchange, Leave by Blackwall Tunnel Northern Approach Southbound, SDOL."

The examiner probed further into my personal life.

"So, coming out of London, Mr. Hutley, you come off the M11 by Bishops Stortford, Exit junction 8?" He was literally like rain man, he probably even knew what I had for breakfast!

"Yes, sir!"

"So that Bishops Stortford area is close to Ugley. Do you know which famous TV chef has a restaurant there?"

"Sorry sir, I don't know who."

"It's Jamie Oliver, do you know of any of his restaurants in London?"

"15, sir, Westland Place."

THE KNOWLEDGE

"Okay, Mr. Hutley, have you been anywhere on holiday this year?"

I had been to a variety of places that year; Dublin, Budapest, but I knew these could spiral into more obscure points, so I decided to give a more solid and closed answer (that I had also been to).

"Dominican Republic, sir". My brain was praying; please ask for the embassy, please ask for the embassy!!!

"Very nice, do they have an embassy in London?"

"Collingham Place, sir!" I replied excitedly, almost before he had finished asking the question.

"Correct, now take me there."

The great advantage of having a bit of talking time between ascertaining points is that it gives you the chance to think about how to leave the start point. Westland Place is very easy to leave and jump onto City Road. This line came pretty much instantly but still proceeding with care, I calmly and confidently called the run out loud for the examiner. So far so good! Two more runs to go.

My current job at the time was as a Barista at Starbucks, so I was asked Starbucks HQ to Frazier St, after the sitcom *Frasier,* which was based in Seattle, where the first Starbucks coffee was located. As it was a nice long run, I opted to call big roads, lowering the number of words I would have to recite and, therefore, minimising my chances of hesitation.

I knew by this point. I had called three fluent and good lines, so I had a chance of success. The examiner gave me one final run; Nelson Square to Wellington Square, a nod to Admiral Nelson and the Duke of Wellington. My mind froze. I knew the line and route to take but I felt hesitant about actually starting to call the run, knowing that it could be the last ever one I would have to call in that chair. It was almost self-sabotage; potentially, the final jump that would

89

APPERANCES

graduate me from a mere Knowledge boy to a London cab driver.

My voice trembling, I slowly called and pieced together the run. Eyes closed in concentration, I could hear the examiner shuffling his papers and opening the cabinet drawers. Maybe he's getting all the documents together to say that I've passed!

"SDOL Kings Road." A long pause.

"Do you go to a Knowledge school, Mr. Hutley?"

"No, sir. I live a bit too far away from a school."

"Well, I would suggest looking into one, you dropped a few points, it might be beneficial to sharpen up your Knowledge of London."

Prior to this appearance, I had only failed two exams. I was adamant this was a scoring exam, maybe he was bluffing, or was I delusional to think that I'd completed The Knowledge of London?

My elbows rested on my knees and my head was crunched forward as I stared at the floor. I'd mentally run a marathon and this position allowed me to catch my breath and gain my composure.

I looked up and saw an open hand stretched over the desk and map, glowing and ready.

"But at this stage, I'm satisfied to say you already have an exceptional Knowledge of London. Well done, Mr. Hutley."

I stood up and the euphoria hit me. I shook his hand and I'm sure the examiner could feel the energy and tension being released through this exchange. Up until now, the experience in this room had been the same, but this time it was finally over!

The examiner gave a few parting comments and went on to explain the next steps. His words became muted as my brain just processed the situation.

THE KNOWLEDGE

It's over, I never had to call another run. A few tears began to flow as I cast my mind back to the beginning stages when it seemed like the most unachievable dream. It was done, it was real. After two years and 10 months of relentless driving, calling and studying, I had finally completed The Knowledge!

"The next time I see you, Mr. Hutley, you will be a London cab driver."

My completed scorecard

APPERANCES

SUBURBAN RUNS

You've maintained the most impossible schedule for several years, reached the required standard and received a handshake from an examiner who, after dozens of appearances, deems you to be worthy of driving a London black taxi. But it's not over yet.

Your formalised examination process that pertains to the six-mile radius of Charing Cross has been completed, and you have now received your "req" and handshake. Nothing can take away that hard work and this factor is set in stone (thank goodness!). But you still have to learn an additional 180 runs. Compared to the extensive work that goes into The Knowledge, this is just a minor bump in the road but nevertheless, it is still a long and respectable task.

The reasoning behind these Suburban runs is to ensure you are able to confidently navigate out of Central London and into various locations of the London Suburbs. You aren't expected to learn the micro level of knowledge that is required for central London, merely learn runs that provide a good understanding of the geography that exists within the M25 radius.

By this point in the process, you should be able to effectively schedule these lengthy runs. For myself, I wanted the process over as soon as possible, so I went out every evening after work and called them every hour under the sun, going from no runs to the completed exam in just three weeks.

It is a required formality, and the best part about this section is that you are under no time pressure to complete it. One friend got his req one month before me (October 2017), but didn't complete his suburbs until four months after I had been driving a cab! (April 2018).

Even throughout The Knowledge, I learnt runs and points best by physically running them. Some people who reach this hurdle believe they can merely learn by reciting the book. Let me tell you, there have been plenty of times in the cab where I've been glad to have actually been to the locations; experience when the appropriate turn comes up etc. You are now a London cab driver, so it is a required standard to at least visit the suburban areas where your potential paying passenger will want to go.

LONDON CAB DRIVER

Me recciving my green badge - December 2017

BADGE DAY

The most unobtainable day. The day you believe will never come. On Monday you sat your final ever exam (suburbs) and by Friday you are collecting the badge you have dreamed about since day one.

Part of the relief of this day is knowing that you will never have to set foot in the exam centre again. You will never have to call over another run. The life you have been dreaming of is outside of the walls you are sat in. You have achieved The Knowledge and you know, through the strong work ethic that you have built, you can achieve absolutely anything life throws at you.

From this point, the world is your oyster, you can rent a cab that evening and get straight to work (as I did), or put your badge in the drawer and pick it up in a years' time. It is the most intensive and drawn out job interview in the world. The best thing is that when you get out to work, the majority of the hard work is done and you already know how to do the job!

RENTING VS. BUYING A CAB

Like renting or buying a house, both options have plenty of advantages and disadvantages when it comes to working the cab.

RENTING A CAB

Advantages

- Easy to dip your toe into work.
- Flexible garage options, rent by the day, weekend, week or long term. Shop around for a garage that suits your needs and location.
- Renting covers your insurance and maintenance. Engine packs up? No problem, the garage sorts it all out for you.

Disadvantages

- Renting generally works out more expensive in the long run (over a five-year span or more)
- You are tied to one garage for your maintenance.
- You are governed by your garage for routine maintenance. My friend has sat through multiple MOTs because he had been given a new cab after coming off holiday, only to be phoned up a week later saying he needs to bring it in for an MOT.

BUYING A CAB

Advantages

- Generally, it's cheaper in the long run and once you have paid it off, your regular expenses drop dramatically.
- You have more control over your cab. You can get a livery (advertisement) on your cab, giving you a nice annual cash boost.

Disadvantages

- You are liable for your own insurance. Hire and reward insurance can be very expensive if you are young or new to the cab trade.
- You pay for your maintenance and downtime. If your engine let's go, not only do you need to pay for the repair, but you can also be out of work by not having a cab!
- You might assume that most older/experienced drivers have their own cab whilst the younger and less experienced drivers rent. This isn't the case, some drivers don't like the stress of having to manage their own cab and like being able to keep their livelihood and overheads simple.

For the foreseeable future, I will be renting my cab. Whilst I am incredibly sensible and budgeted in my personal finance, it is still a great relief to know that if I run into any financial difficulty, all I need to do is take the cab back to the garage and I can stop paying. It is a much bigger commitment if you are tied into a finance deal and it's harder to wriggle out of!

FIRST DAY OUT

A very old and accepted tradition, which brings good luck to a new cab driver, is to provide their first fare for free.

Despite having studied London intensively every day for the past 55 months and having over a dozen gruelling appearances, nothing quite compares to the moment when you are in the cab, badge around your neck, ready to pick up your first paying customer.

I remember driving to an area of London I was most familiar with, the City. In the middle of Smithfield meat market, I finally plucked up the courage to turn my hire light on. I turned left at Long Lane and then sat patiently at the traffic lights opposite Beech Street. Just as the lights turn green, a couple of ladies hailed me down. I quickly beckoned them to jump in the back.

Turning right into Aldersgate Street to move off the traffic lights, I couldn't hear a thing the ladies were saying. There was also a really loud beeping noise! I looked at the dash in the cab and saw the passenger door was slightly open (happens a lot driving the cab). I pulled up to the kerb and asked them to slam the door a bit harder, then figured out they couldn't hear me as I hadn't got the intercom on!

Eventually, I managed to communicate the message to them and they tried to open the door. "It's stuck driver!" they replied. It seemed like everything that could go wrong with this fare was going wrong, thank goodness it was for free! After what felt like an eternity, I remembered that holding your foot on the brake activates the internal locks, so I put the cab into park, released my foot and then, voila, the door became free. Once the hiccup of the door was over, I was then in a better state to hear where they wished to go: "Fore Street please!" After a brief moment of thought, it clicked... it's only around the corner so off we go; F Aldersgate, Comply Rotunda, Lve by L London Wall, L Wood Street, R Fore Street. £3.40. "Don't worry, ladies, the fare is on me!" Of course, it is an incredibly small gesture but they were hugely grateful, the small things in life, eh?

DAY-TO-DAY DRIVER

As much as I like to routine my time doing the job to create consistent working patterns, this job is fabulously inconsistent. I will sometimes head off to work a couple of hours earlier than my set hours; the logic being, the more hours in town, the more money one can earn, when in reality it can go the opposite way. I've had days where I've turned up a couple of hours after my set time and ended up doing better!

It's important to remember that you cannot work all the time. Yes, the fantastic opportunity of this job is that you can work when you want. I believe doing your set hours will lead to a much more routined and fulfilled life. You can chase the money, but ultimately, you will see hours of your life pour away behind the steering wheel. I studied The Knowledge to have a better quality of life, not to waste my days working every hour that I can!

It's been over a year since finishing The Knowledge and I still get a buzz rolling into London in my cab. I love looking down and seeing the shining green badge around my neck, spotting the first hand hailing me at the start of my shift, winding down my window, knowing that I could be asked anywhere in London and would be able to confidently identify the location and know the most efficient route to get there.

The Knowledge doesn't just grant you a badge to work, it makes you the best taxi driver in the world.

GLOSSARY

Appearance - The oral examinations that Knowledge students must progress through to become a London cab driver.

Banana - A wide called line. Self-criticising knowledge students often say, "Woah, I called a banana there!"

Blue Book (BB) - The fundamental books that every Knowledge student begins with and uses to learn The Knowledge. These books contain a total of 320 runs across the capital.

Call over - The process of calling runs with a call-over partner, this can be done at school or at home, but both must be carried out in front of the map.

Call-over partner (COP) - Another Knowledge boy or girl who you take turns with to recite runs. Call-over partners pen and spot mistakes in the other student's called line.

Comply (COM) - To go around/go through, usually used on roundabouts or busy junctions. "Forward Lambeth Road, Comply Lambeth Circus, Leave by Lambeth Palace Road".

Drop a point - When a point of interest is not known, thereby dropping the point (and quite literally losing a point in your potential score during an exam).

GLOSSARY

Getting your drop - When you move up to the next examination stage. Advancing from 56's to 28's would be an example of "getting your drop to 28's".

Illegal - A manoeuvre or route that is not allowed to be used, such as SDOR when there is a central reservation in the way, calling a one-way street the wrong way, or calling a banned no right turn.

Knowledge boy/girl - Someone who is studying the knowledge. The term is still applicable regardless of age, i.e. a man in his fifties is still termed as a "Knowledge boy".

LOL/LOR - Leave on left/leave on right. Refers to which direction the cab is oriented when you leave the point in accordance with the flow of traffic. For instance, at the British Museum; LOL would mean your direction is eastbound on Great Russell Street, while LOR would mean you're leaving direction is westbound on Great Russell Street.

Oranges and Lemons - Big roads on the map. This refers to the colours used on the A-Z map, keeping a line simple could be referred to as "sticking to the oranges and lemons".

Outpointed - When the Knowledge student drops multiple points in an appearance, usually resulting in a D, they have been outpointed by the examiner.

Pass out - Getting your badge and completing The Knowledge, you pass out of The Knowledge process.

PCO - Public Carriage Office, 210 Blackfriars Road, where examinations take place.

Penning - When a called route is drawn/penned on the map. This is to visually reinforce the route/line in the student's memory.

Point - A point of interest. Each run usually features two points, a start and end point.

THE KNOWLEDGE

Point to Point - The process of calling runs, from one point to another, usually performed with runs from a sheet or random points.

Redlined - When a student has accumulated four D's/failures on a given appearance level, they have to restart the level. Two consecutive redlines on the same level pushes the candidate back to the preceding level.

Req - The completion of your final exam, achieving your requisition to become a cab driver. Often known as reaching the required standard and finishing the majority section of The Knowledge.

Ring of Fire - The chairs in the waiting area directly outside of the examination rooms at 210 Blackfriars Road.

Run - A route from one point of interest to another.

SDOL/SDOR - Set Down on Left/Set Down on Right.

Sheet - Daily point sheets produced by schools. These are emailed around 3pm on working weekdays to subscribers and feature runs that have been asked by examiners that day.

TfL - Transport for London. The governing body of London's extensive transport networks, as well as taxis and The Knowledge.

Turnaround - A legal method of leaving a point of interest to spin the cab in the opposite direction. This usually involves a "turnaround", featuring a few streets/roads that allow for this process in the shortest/most efficient manner possible.

KNOWLEDGE SCHOOLS & RESOURCES

These resources were helpful to me on The Knowledge. This is not a prescription as we all learn differently. I believe in covering all bases and becoming as immersed as possible in order to maximise your best chances of success.

Anki Flashcard App - https://apps.ankiweb.net - The flashcard app I personally used on The Knowledge.

Eleanor Cross Knowledge School - http://eleanorcross.net - Features good mock exams and I subscribed to their daily sheets.

Knowledge Point - http://www.taxitradepromotions.co.uk - One of the original Knowledge schools, I attended their eight-week "Compass Course".

Licensed Taxi Driver Association (LTDA) – http://www.ltda.co.uk – The largest union in the London taxi trade,

StormCab - http://www.stormcab.com - Useful cab driver resources.

KNOWLEDGE SCHOOLS & RESOURCES

Taxi Knowledge of London Facebook group - https://www.facebook.com/groups/51842496979/ - Useful for finding call-over partners and staying up to date with the latest road restrictions.

The Knowledge: The World's Toughest Taxi Test - https://www.channel4.com/programmes/the-knowledge-the-worlds-toughest-taxi-test - Broadcast April 2017. A documentary that includes footage of Knowledge students at various stages of The Knowledge.

Transport for London - https://tfl.gov.uk/info-for/taxis-and-private-hire/licensing/learn-the-knowledge-of-london (Contains numerous Knowledge schools).

View from the mirror blog - Robert Lordan - https://blackcablondon.net – Includes an entertaining recollection of Robert's journey on The Knowledge.

WizAnn - https://www.wizann.co.uk - WizAnn have numerous Knowledge apps. I personally used WizBooks to store and revise my Blue Book runs.

Printed in Dunstable, United Kingdom